Struik Publishers (Pty) Ltd
(a member of Struik New Holland Publishing)
80 McKenzie Street
Cape Town 8001
Reg. No.: 54/00965/07

ISBN 1 86872 166 3

Reproduction: Hirt & Carter, Cape Town
Printing: National Book Printers, Goodwood

FRONT COVER *A typical spring flower display.*

SPINE Crassula columnaris

BACK COVER Grielum humifusum

TITLE PAGE *One of Namaqualand's spring-
flowering bulbs,* Lapeirousia silenoides, *flowers in granite rock crevices.*

RIGHT Grielum humifusum *and the rain
daisy* Dimorphotheca pluvialis *flower on the
coastal plain inland from Port Nolloth.*

INTRODUCTION

Namaqualand's major attraction, its springtime floral spectacle, is recognised as one of the world's natural wonders. But this dry region in the northwest corner of South Africa has much more to offer the visitor. It is a land of wide open skies and huge panoramas, and its stark beauty is nowhere greater than in the mountains of the Richtersveld – the most arid part of the region. The journey from Cape Town along the Cape West Coast, through the Olifants River Valley, past the Cedarberg mountains, and through Namaqualand provides the traveller with a fascinating change of landscape and the chance to enjoy an extraordinary variety of flowering plants.

LEFT Daisies carpet a Kamiesberg fruit orchard in early spring, before the trees blossom.
OVERLEAF In spring, daisies like these gazanias Gazania krebsiana *(RIGHT) cover the granite hills overlooking Langebaan lagoon (LEFT).*

LEFT A fisherman's cottage at St. Helena Bay, on the Cape West Coast, is surrounded by a natural garden.

At Clanwilliam, en route *to Namaqualand,*
visitors to the wild flower garden (OPPOSITE)
in the Ramskop Nature Reserve can enjoy
many of the flowers from surrounding areas
as well as some of the birds, like this male
malachite sunbird (RIGHT) perched on a rocket
pincushion Leucospermum reflexum. *This*
pincushion grows naturally in the nearby
Cedarberg mountains.

In spring, the Ramskop wild flower garden puts on a brilliant show, which includes annual daisies such as Arctotis fastuosa *(RIGHT) and bokbaaivygies (ice-plants,* Dorotheanthus bellidiformis) *(OPPOSITE).*

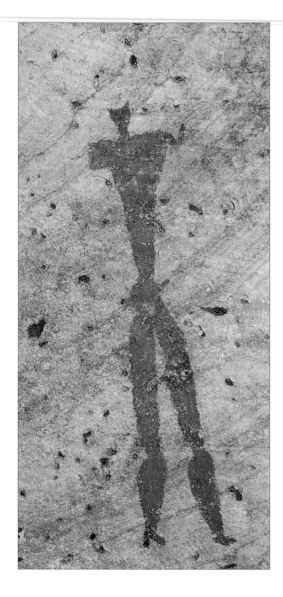

OPPOSITE, LEFT AND ABOVE The Cedarberg mountains contain many examples of fine Khoisan rock art, well preserved and in good condition because of the dry climate.

OVERLEAF With the peaks of the Cedarberg as a backdrop, rain daisies Dimorphotheca pluvialis *cover a fallow field on a farm north of Clanwilliam.*

Wild flowers like the Namaqualand daisy *Dimorphotheca sinuata (LEFT) are not all that the Olifants River Valley has to offer. During winter and early spring the citrus orchards (OPPOSITE), which line the river here, yield their splendid bounty.*
OVERLEAF The Biedouw Valley, tucked behind the Cedarberg mountains beyond Clanwilliam, can put on an entrancing springtime display, and it is well worth making a detour to enjoy its splendours.

LEFT AND OPPOSITE Nieuwoudtville is situated on the Bokkeveld Escarpment, which looks west over Namaqualand's arid Knersvlakte. The spring flowering here is particularly colourful with a varied range of species not encountered in Namaqualand.

LEFT *At Nieuwoudtville, spring is not the only spectacular season. Here, autumn-flowering candelabra flowers* Brunsvigia bosmaniae *shine* en masse *in the light of the moon rising over dolerite koppies.*

The glory of Nieuwoudtville's floral richness is its wealth of beautiful bulbs (OPPOSITE), often seen flowering among the annuals.

Two of these treasures are Lapeirousia oreogena *(RIGHT) and the harlequin flower* Sparaxis tricolor *(ABOVE).*

The autumn-flowering river lily Crinum variabile *(LEFT) grows above the Nieuwoudt-ville waterfall (OPPOSITE). Sparaxis elegans (BELOW) is another of Nieuwoudtville's floral specials.*

The quartz pebble patches which dot the Knersvlakte are a treasure trove of dwarf succulents such as Conophytum calculus *(OPPOSITE, LEFT)*, Crassula columnaris *(OPPOSITE, RIGHT)* and Drosanthemum schoenlandianum *(ABOVE)*. Bushman candles Monsonia crassicaule *(LEFT)* are widespread throughout Namaqualand.

Quartz pebble patches in the Knersvlakte
support Argyroderma crateriforme *(ABOVE),*
Oophytum nanum *(RIGHT), and the rare*
babiana Babiana *sp. (OPPOSITE).*

Aloe variegata (RIGHT) is one of the small aloes found in Namaqualand, its name describing the distinct patterning on its leaves. This plant, and the mesemb Argyroderma fissum *(OPPOSITE), grow on the red soils of the Knersvlakte.*

OVERLEAF The Knersvlakte is probably best known for its striking displays of spring annuals seen against the backdrop of the Matsikamma, Gifberg and Bokkeveld Escarpment mountains.

The rural people of Namaqualand lead an unsophisticated, often hard existence. The descendants of the Khoi-Khoi occasionally still live in traditional reed huts (matjieshutte) (ABOVE).

These homes are built over a frame of saplings, which is abandoned when the people and their herds of goats move on, often in donkey carts (OPPOSITE), to better pastures.

The exposed granite faces of the hills (klipkoppe) and mountains are a characteristic feature of Namaqualand inland from the coastal plain and north of the Knersvlakte. This farm (OPPOSITE) lies on the slopes of the region's highest mountains, the Kamiesberg. Working mules (ABOVE) are one of the familiar sights of Namaqualand.

OVERLEAF, LEFT Bat-eared foxes are fairly common in Namaqualand but, because they are active only at night – except in the coldest months – they are not often seen. These delightful creatures are insect-eaters.
OVERLEAF, RIGHT Namaqualand is home to several tortoise species, including the angulate tortoise.

Monkey beetles mating on Gazania krebsiana *(OPPOSITE), and a muscid fly feeding on* Ruschia sp. *(ABOVE). The grasshopper perching on* Romulea namaquensis *(LEFT) is just a visitor.*

LEFT *Because of its limited annual rainfall, the greater part of Namaqualand is uncultivated. Wheat, however, is grown on the higher lying land between Bitterfontein and Kamieskroon, and sheep, here shown grazing a fallow field, are widely farmed.*

Previously cultivated land in the Goegap Nature Reserve (ABOVE) and in the Skilpad Reserve (OPPOSITE), is the ideal habitat for annuals which provide the splashes of bright colour in Namaqualand's spring landscape.

OVERLEAF Annuals, mainly colourful daisies (RIGHT) and bulbs such as Babiana framesii *(LEFT), are the types of plants which contribute most to Namaqualand's mass displays of colour in spring.*

The mass flowering (LEFT) of annuals such as Gazania lichtensteinii (ABOVE) in spring is just part of their survival strategy. Annuals have to germinate, grow, flower and produce seed in the few short months of winter and early spring before they die in the heat of summer, surviving only in seed form until the start of the next cycle.

Bulbs such as Babiana curviscapa *(LEFT) survive Namaqualand's hot, dry summers by retreating below ground. After flowering in spring, the leaves and flowers die off, leaving the bulb to put out new growth when (and if) water becomes available during the following autumn and winter. Perennial plants, like the mesemb bushes flowering here among annual daisies (OPPOSITE), survive the stress of summer by storing water in their succulent leaves or stems.*

*ABOVE AND OPPOSITE In good years, annuals such as these daisies germinate,
grow and flower so prolifically that they pack every available space.*

Crossyne flava *(RIGHT) is one of the autumn flowering amaryllids. These bulbs avoid competing with other plants for insect pollinators by flowering when few other species do. They put up leaves and grow in the winter rainy season after their flowerheads have died off.*

OPPOSITE A quiver tree Aloe dichotoma *dominates a stormy spring landscape in the Goegap Nature Reserve.*

OVERLEAF Grielum humifusum *and daisies flower amongst the granite boulders of the Klipkoppe (LEFT). This is also the habitat of the mesemb* Conicosia elongata *(RIGHT), a perennial with a large, fleshy underground tuber relished by porcupines.*

LEFT Didelta carnosa *is a common daisy along Namaqualand's coast. The soft-winged flower beetle is one of its pollinators. Its seed capsules are covered with spikes to aid dispersal – when animals tread on them, the capsules are picked up and carried a distance before they are dropped again. Bee-flies pollinate* Lampranthus hoerleinianus *(OPPOSITE) and many other mesembs.*

Some mesembs, such as Monilaria monili-
formis, *can survive on the rocky outcrops
along Namaqualand's coast* (OPPOSITE).
*A slightly more hospitable habitat for flowers
are the limy sandflats* (LEFT), *typical of much
of this coastline.*

Oxalis eckloniana *(ABOVE) grows on the sandy flats of the coastal plain near the Groenrivier mouth. This is also the area in which one of the most spectacular mesembs,* Cephalophyllum spongiosum *(OPPOSITE) flourishes.*

Vegetated dunes line long stretches of Nama-qualand's Atlantic seaboard (OPPOSITE). The Oograbies Hills, which jut out of the coastal plain inland from Port Nolloth, support many small succulents, including Crassula brevifolia (ABOVE) and Cotyledon orbiculata (RIGHT).

Typical of the wealth of dwarf plants which grow in the crevices of the quartzitic rock of the Oograbies Hills are Conophytum meyeri *(LEFT) and* Gazania heterochaeta *(ABOVE).*

Othonna sedifolia *(RIGHT)*, *is a succulent* *perennial daisy and* Ornithogalum osmynellum *(ABOVE)*, *a tiny bulb which* *grows naturally only in these hills.*

The Richtersveld, in the north of Namaqualand, is a region of stark and awesome
beauty. It is the driest part of Namaqualand
despite the presence of the Orange River, its
northern boundary. The plants here, like the
endemic tree aloe Aloe pillansii (OPPOSITE),
have to endure long periods of drought, very
high temperatures and desiccating winds.
The other tall tree aloe, the quiver tree Aloe
dichotoma (LEFT), is more widespread in
Namaqualand and also further afield in
South Africa.

OVERLEAF The arid mountains of the Richtersveld are high – rising over 1 000 m above the
Orange River and the coastal plain – and the
vistas that unfold from the upper slopes are
breathtaking. The plants of the sun-baked lower
reaches of the Richtersveld depend for moisture
on mist banks that roll in periodically from the
cold Atlantic to the west.

When the Richtersveld does have good winter rains – which is seldom – the landscape is transformed. After the rain, the display of flowers on the top of the Helskloof Pass contrasts magically with the distant view of the arid badlands of Namibia (OPPOSITE). Conophytum wettsteinii (LEFT) is one of the dwarf succulents which have evolved to cope with the rigours of the Richtersveld's harsh climate.

OVERLEAF The carrion flower Hoodia gordonii, a plant adapted to extreme drought, produces a putrid scent to attract the flies which pollinate it.